THE OPENING RITUAL

A dazzling lyricist of dawnlight and psalms, G.C. Waldrep inhabits a contemporary devotional mode to explore the flesh as a site of pain yet an instrument of beauty and ecstasy. In the richly scriptural cosmos of *The Opening Ritual* — simultaneously hermeneutical and reflexive — the Holy Spirit is a vowel, and pain is a mineral we store in our bodies. This book is not for the faint of hearts as Waldrep embraces both doubt and healing as components of "faith's torsion." *The Opening Ritual* glows like a bronze retablo and sings like a golden harp, blessing its earthbound subjects with heavenly inspiration.

—KAREN AN-HWEI LEE

In *The Opening Ritual,* G.C. Waldrep's third collection in a trilogy centered on illness and healing, "prophecy has implicated the body." Much like the poem, the body holds its entire trajectory at once, refusing to collapse wound and suture, illness and remission. With a future that is becoming increasingly hard to face, Waldrep reminds us that "the reparations the body seeks / rest in time," and so does its preparations. These poems do not promise to heal what cannot be healed; instead, pain and relief harmonize on the poet's animal tongue. Like no other poet I know, Waldrep returns the word to its origin in ritual, a "place of coming & becoming," where care is not an impossible cure, but a poultice of words we would otherwise be unable to hear.

—SASHA STEENSEN

G. C. Waldrep's *The Opening Ritual* beholds transcendent structures of faith through the glass of the particular and the eccentric. In poems that are in themselves devotional exercises, the poet sloughs off the excrescence of the contemporary moment to reveal a far vaster "sadness of time." A pilgrim wanderer through historic and prehistoric landscapes, Waldrep opens himself to all forms of thought and association, drawing a pattern of thinking from patient sensual observance: from the barely visible and audible, the latent image, the hidden window. All is put at the disposal of the spiritual life.

The collection concludes with a sequence of truly grand meditations on spiritual consciousness — in one the poet notes how, in the stillness of contemplation, the world begins to hum and resound with music. *The Opening Ritual* attends to and fashions its song from that music.

—SASHA DUGDALE

If it's true, as Kierkegaard once posited, that we can only understand life backward but are doomed to live it forward, then our whole lives happen inside an inscrutable now we can never really perceive. Such is the crisis of G.C. Waldrep's *The Opening Ritual,* where lips "silky like ground pearls mixed with oil" whisper into the hopeless enterprise of naming what can be named before it slips back off into air or mud. "I have not written sufficiently of earth, and of the things of earth," Waldrep says, recalling—or repudiating—Rilke's Ninth Duino Elegy ("Praise the world to the angel, not the unutterable world..."). A short poem here called "Saint Sauveur" ends in two of the most memorable stanzas I've read in ages, kaleidoscopic in their irreducible clarity, while other poems ("I Am the Vine," "Suite for A.W.N. Pugin") sprawl epically, digress, worry themselves into uncanny incantations buckling their own lyric into something like—dare I say it—purpose? *The Opening Ritual* is the kind of furiously curious, unabashedly ambitious poetry book I want to show everyone, to prove such books can still be written. "I am fully present, but also insufficiently," Waldrep writes. How has it never been said?

—KAVEH AKBAR

ALSO BY G.C. WALDREP
PUBLISHED BY TUPELO PRESS

Archicembalo

Winner of the Dorset Prize

"Often breathtaking in its erudition, at other times imbued with a forceful
simplicity, tricky in its sensibility yet clearly driven by affection, this collection
from Waldrep might be the best book of prose poems to appear in a long while."
— *Publishers Weekly*

feast gently

*Winner of the William Carlos Williams Award
from the Poetry Society of America*

"The poems in G.C. Waldrep's collection, *feast gently,* transcend any fixed ideas
one might have about craft: form, technique, style, voice, tone—and makes
pointless anything one might say in prose about poetry. In this work, each poem,
each line, each choice made seems predetermined, absolute, definitive." — Laura
Kasischke for the Poetry Society

The Earliest Witnesses

"There's no one writing like Waldrep. He is an original. This is
a visionary book."
—*Los Angeles Review of Books*

THE OPENING RITUAL

G.C. Waldrep

TUPELO PRESS
North Adams, Massachusetts

TUPELO PRESS
P.O. Box 1767
North Adams, Massachusetts 01247
(413) 664-9611 / Fax: (413) 664-9711
editor@tupelopress.org / www.tupelopress.org

Tupelo Press is an award-winning independent literary press that publishes fine fiction, non-fiction, and poetry in books that are a joy to hold as well as read. Tupelo Press is a registered 501(c)(3) non-profit organization, and we rely on public support to carry out our mission of publishing extraordinary work that may be outside the realm of the large commercial publishers. Financial donations are welcome and are tax deductible.

This project is supported in part by an award
from the National Endowment for the Arts

CONTENTS

I Have Touched His Wealth With the Certainty of Experience   3

Watching the Flower-Arrangers In Ripon Cathedral   4

Houses Built from the Bodies of Lions or of Dogs   8

On the Senses   10

Suite For A.W.N. Pugin   13

The Holy Spirit as a Vowel In Early Snow (I)   20

Effigy Mounds National Monument   22

[The Healing Loom]   26

Mount Grace Priory   27

Deposition   28

Fountains Abbey, Pentecost   32

Creation Myth Suite   35

Acadia Winter Poem   41

Saint Sauveur   45

Bell Buoy, Otter Cliffs   47

Contemplating the Pippa Blackall Millennium Window
    at Alpheton Church, St. Padarn's Day 2021   48

The Holy Spirit as a Vowel In Early Snow (II)   51

To a Shelf Fungus in Acadia National Park   53

At The George Caleb Bingham House, Arrow Rock, Missouri   57

Tarry   59

And the Stonesquarers   61

Grievance   67

I Am the Vine   70

To Each Light of Which I Am a Brother   73

In the Epoch of Bronze   76

The Arrhythmias   77

Canto Selah   81

A Meadowlark in Arrow Rock, Missouri   82

Suffering   84

The Holy Spirit as a Vowel In Early Snow (III)   86

Exodus   88

Some Lines Written in Clare Priory Yard   89

Marching Bear Group   93

Afternoon Snow, Collegeville   98

In the Designed Landscape (Garden of Planes)   100

Notes & Acknowledgments   *105*

THE OPENING RITUAL

I HAVE TOUCHED HIS WEALTH
WITH THE CERTAINTY OF EXPERIENCE

—Simone Weil

Body of a young hare quite dead lying in a corner
of the pasture. It wasn't there yesterday.
A magpie alights, worries it a bit. The magpie's head
in quick shakes, left & right, its sharp beak
performing the opening ritual. It does this five or six
times before flying away. The first thing the dead
lose are their eyes, failed prophets
with the élan of things that only happen twice.
Love always uses us as if we were infinite, it seems,
although it must know, by now, that we're not.

WATCHING THE FLOWER-ARRANGERS
IN RIPON CATHEDRAL

Let's be strict about what mercy is. It's asking everyone
to STAY WHERE YOU ARE for approximately three minutes
("Thank you for your time"). It's the one woman
holding carnations in her hands & handing them one by one
to the other woman on the stepladder. From somewhere
in the choir a baby wails. We were strangers here, we continue
to be strangers here, a sustained articulation, as of space
constrained. The decision which surfaces light
should be permitted to sluice across—likewise one of the stricter
signatures of mercy. It seems the first woman will never
run out of flowers. Perhaps there is a bucket at her feet.
We were empire. A spear passed through the stippled flank
of our animal dreams, our rhythmic reason. Did you say
"the cruelty of animals" or "an animal cruelty," I no longer
recall. Now stand back & admire the result, little suns
chasing a dog down a narrow street at dusk. Adjust as necessary.
Music has washed down the pavements & this is enough
for one day. Unfortunately, there are other days.
A model of a model of a model once again, inside a church,
the ancient sacristy. Did I mention I was a stranger? The same
three steps upward, now both women trying to add more
blossoms, one on the stepladder, one on the ground. Blind heat,
a branding iron that heals (though it leaves a cauterized scar).
Standing & holding not a piece of inflamed silk, knowing
that someone else is present to lift lightning from your grasp.
The empty hand that hovers over the hour & just under
the lidded eye. With what scrutiny do the vestments of others
enter our lives, scaffolds the thieves climb up
& down, continuously. Now the flowers come thicker, faster,

4

carnations, roses, daisies—all yellow, some obviously dyed.
I fail to locate the retablo showing the saint in the act
of cauterizing (the guidebook does not specify whether his own
flesh or the flesh of some other). Would you apply fire
to your own flesh, to the flesh of someone you love,
to the flesh of a stranger? If you thought it would heal, or if
you thought it would wound? Because I am standing right here.
I have had some ideas about war, & about the pity of war.
My long bones have decided to acknowledge gravity,
to grin at it. Throw the bouquet, madonna of the underlying
gypsum strata. A little water & anything, everything
could disappear into the void. When I say "void"
I mean deixis, the act of pointing, three steps up to the plane
where mercy is reconstituting itself (with a little help).
This may or may not be a building in which no one has died,
I can't know. I sketch the year in which my patrimony
was taken from me. It looks almost like a hospital. —Well.
It *is* a hospital! I thought it was just a sketch. The afflicted
lurch into & out of it in miniature while I watch. One by one
the wreaths are hoisted. The wreaths cast no shadows,
is this some trick of the light? There is no sense in anger
as there is no "sense" in prophecy, as such. Prophecy, as such,
led me here. I sweep the birds from the worn flags,
they ring like struck brass & then break into microscopic
fragments. How I coveted a bright, bright tongue.
Or a painting of a tongue. Nations slept through the film
of God's indifference. Let's decorate the hospital with artworks
by children, their sly dissimulations. Map me, three
steps up, three steps back down. A man in a sky-blue cassock

places a book just so, among all the other books.
Everything ceases to be real only when you pay for it:
this is why nations go to war. I admit I did not care for war,
or so I thought (I was naive about this, as about so many things).
More flowers brought from a back room—this goes on & on.
It must be the eve of some festival, some commemoration.
The difference between a prophet & a martyr
has to do with war, perhaps. And nations. To set a fire
in this holy place, to film someone setting a fire: an idea,
I mean, that one could have. A still from the montage.
Let's say it's the nation's combust having been left behind
in a forest clearing. It was carried there. It was (or wasn't)
very small. It looked charred like a break in a song.
Poor song! Poor plenitude, you are dismissed—no, sorry,
I can't help you. Always the same woman on the stepladder,
always the same woman on the ground, handing up flowers.
Green, green, & gold, famished passage of the octaves.
The parchment of treachery, carelessly pricked
by the apprentice's stylus: what will you record here
with your thunder & your debts? Will you tape it to your biceps,
to your forehead, like a target to the small of your back.
Invite the men to admire the work, yes (the women do).
Force them down on all fours, to pick up any leftover flowers
I presume. I presume a great deal, I know. This could
be something else, a rite, a dance, a sacrifice. An accident.
The time I fell into the keeping of the state, & of its knives.
The machine they forced upon me. It was not a dance,
I remember thinking that much. No one filmed,

no one took any photographs. What I am recording now
could be false even though I witnessed it. You have placed
yourself in the hands of a stranger, hands that are strung
with wire like some musical instrument. They measure you.
They measure the width of the display our piety exerts.
I would get down on all fours myself, but my spine
no longer permits that particular obeisance. Instead let's talk
about doors. Some of the doors are hung with wreaths,
others are blocked entirely by floral displays. Isn't this
how it is, always, with the doors. Some of them
may not be doors at all, like the ghostly link between *participle*
& *participate*. I am reminded again of the fable in which
the fox is deceived into addressing a hedge of roses.
"My friends, my friends" the fox keeps saying, but somehow
he can't go any further. He had even washed his paws
for the occasion. Once more I consider the etymology
of *glisten*. I've broken the ark of sleep into so many pieces
I can no longer tell them apart. I'd like to think
they sing at dusk. But this isn't that, this is about what's real,
what I'm watching right now, what I'm not making up:
the women & men, the flowers, all I'm capable of
apprehending. When one's altar is a flame one either
worships the flame or one measures it. I dream in pain
& I wake in pain. Pain is a mineral. We store it in our bodies.
I hand mine to the next man, his foot already on the rung.

HOUSES BUILT FROM THE BODIES OF LIONS OR OF DOGS

I went to an island off the coast of a continent two islands actually almost neighbors.

On one it was summer on the other winter (snow blowing rain sleet etc.).

Either way the weather was my confession I must have signed for it with my other name.

What was my other name I can't recall but perhaps it was Time.

Very early rising on either island the sun like a thousand beds (somebody else's) on fire.

On the one island I read Augustine on the other I read Mechthild.

On the one island I saw the spare bones whitening on the other I did not.

This was to be a poem of creatures but creatures merely inspire a desire to photograph.

And yes we are so tired of hearing about photography in poems.

It has become the 20th-century equivalent of the soul (in poems) only now it's the 21st.

Easy enough to consider photography an evolution of the soul especially photos of animals.

You have seen these before close-up of a pigeon faded sepia of sheep milling about.

Silhouette of a dog (and a man) above a rock presumably on the one island both long dead now.

I think of dogs the same way as I think of the law i.e. something we've domesticated.

Or not quite but when we call it comes especially if it is hungry and we seem kind.

Then we can make the law (the dog) do less kind things to others once we've fed it satisfied
    its lusts.

So I fed law on one of the islands (can't recall which) and then I was at a loss.

I read Augustine on one of the islands (the first) and disliked him more with every page.

It is one thing to think of language as shiny another to palpate it like a cankered tongue.

Mechthild on the other hand is obsessed with courtly love and counting often at the same time.

She says things like The bride has a crimson silk cloth which is hope.

She writes chapter titles like God's Singing Response to the Soul in Five Things.

She asserts Then the sweet wounds shall heal as though a rose petal had been placed on the spot of the wound.

Vanity takes such diverse forms I thought on the second island watching it snow.

I tried to take photographs of the snow in the same way I try to take photographs of my body.

But God builds His house with His mouth says Mechthild who should know.

Well that is better than God building His house from the bodies of lions or of dogs.

It is not difficult to remember when the doctor first suggested shock therapy.

A possibility he said polishing his glasses with care then he said it again A possibility.

Possibilities are what make you stand still suddenly in the snow letting it rest on your exposed flesh.

That is possibilities are a moment of perception of realizing God is watching (you).

That is possibilities require the perceiver to put the camera down.

You are at the center of something and language is suddenly a flashing milk.

Breath is your companion you pet it you stroke its matted fur affectionately.

You can see this in the photograph Mechthild peeking shyly from behind the damaged lens.

She has gotten the exposure right she has captured on film God's mouth building.

My breath rushes joyfully to greet her places its paws on her narrow shoulders.

This is how I tell the islands apart on one I am dreaming on the other I make mistakes.

On one I could see the sea from my bed on the other I simply knew it was there.

ON THE SENSES

Mount Desert

Mechthild says
the senses
are where anyone
may speak:
God, the devil,
& all creatures.

I stood
in the garden
of my soul
& closed my eyes.

Men toiled
to grade roads
for the carriages
of the wealthy
here. Their works
last awhile.

I strode
in silence, a stiff
breeze whipping
whitecaps
on the surface
of the clear pond.

I rejoiced, at last,
in the decrepitude
of my body.

Concerning
burned love,
Mechthild wrote.

Concerning
the hunger cloth.

Speak then,
Mercator. Shake
the ash
from your lips,
like ground pearls
mixed with oil.

The freshness.
I watched a maple
steam gently
in the dawnlight.

Sip
from the fossil
threading the
temple's shadow.

The wind chalks it
up, & then
back down again—

recidivist,
skeined as
though for psalm.

SUITE FOR A.W.N. PUGIN

PUGIN

I was reading a biography of Pugin. Architecture
was how Pugin avoided God.
This much is evident. When he slipped out at night
to drift down to the water he was a smoke.
He did not look up at the moon. We can be sure
that any bargain he made was intentional
especially those he bound in straps made of snow.

PUGIN

I was reading a biography of Pugin. Exile
is something like a hearse is something, tungsten
or zinc. You are born through it. Some few
emerge from that labor wearing something
their lovers, later, will call a caul. "Look, a caul"
they will say. But they will be wrong about that.
Later they will dream of the circus on fire.

PUGIN

I was reading a biography of Pugin. Funny
that at one point he should have fancied himself
a maker of chairs, when actually
he was a student of gravity. So much gravity!
he said to himself on his walks. What can I bid
for it. What tract can I force into its hand.
Gravity: it is a debt I suspect incurred by God.

PUGIN

I was reading a biography of Pugin, who took
a cloud and rolled it up and sliced it into
equal segments, minor arcs. He offered these
to the choristers who had gathered around him.
He hated being watched while he worked
so he planed their sockets out. He made them
so smooth even music couldn't wake them.

PUGIN

I was reading a biography of Pugin that did not
mention John Clare. Not once.
This must have been an oversight. John Clare
sleeping fitfully in the hedgerows, visions of Mary
flashing across his torn scalp like blueprints.
All the wounded soldiers confined to the hospital.
Do not doubt he knew those angles, their shatter.

PUGIN

I was reading a biography of Pugin. Devotion
is something that takes shape, sometimes
in one medium, sometimes another. This is the key
to understanding how evil slips in. Evil recognizes
the lock but has no concept of error.
It is we who impute error. But a building
is not a metaphor and so Pugin tries hard not to.

PUGIN

I was reading a biography of Pugin who in youth
admired the theater so much he slept
with it. This makes sense, the sex of course
but also his work with set design. Bind your eyes
and then tell me what the theater *feels* like, you
can use any other body part or natural faculty
to inform your answer which must be in French.

PUGIN

I was reading a biography of Pugin in advance
of travel to a far country where once in the past
I had been mistaken for a reenactor. *Snip snip*
went the shears in the abbey lanary which is
a spondee if you like. It was a woman and her child
who saw me crossing an ancient bridge
in steady rain. They had their question marks on.

PUGIN

I was reading a biography of Pugin who stopped
writing his novel about Pan in the wilderness
after spotting himself in one of Turner's paintings.
This was in London, everything choked on smog.
You can't get out that way the ticket-taker
kept trying to admonish, a red spur stoking her voice.
But we pressed ahead towards the police barrier.

PUGIN

I was reading a biography of Pugin. Now wounds
cast their bitter crowns into the river.
Now I retranslate from Book II of the Aeneid.
H.G. Wells lives in the flat where sorrow dwelt.
He has improved it considerably, note these damask
curtains which is what the future tastes like.
This is the sound matter makes greeting matter.

PUGIN

I was reading a biography of Pugin who, based
on available evidence, never carried his father
on his back. Never stood up inside a war and shouted
"Proust." Never pretended to be a tree on fire.
All the silver arrows were naked in the night quarry.
It would have been easy for him to have gathered
them. It would have been easy, but he didn't.

PUGIN

I was reading a biography of Pugin when a knock
at the door reminded me I had not
washed the handshake of God from my forearm
which being very large He had grasped
by mistake. So I did that. Choirs sang large
casks of daylight into the meadow where the girl
had died after being struck by lightning.

PUGIN

I was reading a biography of Pugin in a tree-shaped
cave. Men and women pushed past me
bearing both gifts. I mixed the ingredients
and then listened but the cave was silent and I
was no longer sure of my relation to law. The law
was silent too. We were silent together.
This is sometimes how it is in the tree-shaped cave.

PUGIN

I was reading a biography of Pugin, it was time
for the banquet of forms, I lowered all the blinds.
Look I know you say it was a woman
but how would you know if you did not touch her.
I did not say I did not touch her.
All the black cars were parked in pain's street.
All the black dogs inside, matted pelts.

PUGIN

I was reading a biography of Pugin, who once
tried to build a church in the shape of a thorn.
What a great idea! glass said.
It was hot to the touch. Paint the bones black.
You won't have to read Augustine anymore.
There will be a separate door for shadows to use.
We will dress like planets in winter, you and I.

PUGIN

I was reading a biography of Pugin when I realized
it had been ten days since I had heard music,
any kind of music. My justice had LAW written
all over it. It was sharp the way kings are sharp.
I bathed it lovingly in disinfectant
which dried almost immediately when I lifted it
towards where the wound was feeding on silence.

PUGIN

I was reading a biography of Pugin in summer
which is like a lion kept imprisoned in a small cage
in a village that has forgotten it exists.
No one feeds it. No one waters it. Somehow
the lion does not die. Then one day it does (die).
This is the sort of drama that makes a nation
tell another nation how strong it is, how powerful.

PUGIN

I was reading a biography of Pugin when the finch
flew into the church, and then back out again.
This is either good luck or bad luck, depending.
I declared myself a school and opened myself to war.
War learned a great deal inside me, I think.
I think this because I have read war's memoir.
I make the most of its elisions and obscurities.

PUGIN

I was reading a biography of Pugin in search of
what others call ghosts. *Myself myself*
I thought the refugees were saying. (I was wrong.)
The river tumbling like a pair of glasses
in hot sun. The soul is a nut God dreams of.
He cracks it (in His dream). Shyly falling out
onto the warm sand, every smooth version of us.

PUGIN

I was reading a biography of Pugin. The lamps
came on, indicating dusk. It did not feel
like dusk. It felt like the war in the Balkans
but that was years ago. I began to evolve a theory
of dusk, which like Lazarus rises
when God tells it to. Its sisters are jealous.
They had been famous for a little while, you see.

THE HOLY SPIRIT AS A VOWEL
IN EARLY SNOW (I)

And the spirit was in the wheels, they moved
straight forward.

We raise the future
as if from a deep well, hand over hand.
The future is dark & wet like well water &
sings in me, a weakness.

Staring into the mouth of that inconstancy
gathering in the coulees at dusk.

We are exhausted from all this motion, true:
the algebras & analects. Prophecy, what
have you done to us, you conspirator, you
have implicated the body.
One day is the dream of the next, the next.

I thank you, great city of the north.
I thank you, great cities of the archipelagoes,
your syncopes & disarmaments.

For we are mirrors of division, blood
oranges, pomegranates
in season: here, my sharp knife, wield it.

Gratitude, that ministry, embrace of what
others already know. Mastery,
an affliction, like the captions of my nights,

the churning light of them, a confluence,
a name. *Be quick, be quick, be quick*
the juncos admonish.

They (the wheels)
moved straight forward, across the plain.

EFFIGY MOUNDS NATIONAL MONUMENT

Harpers Ferry, Iowa

I had not realized my breath had no champion, here.
The winding avenues, earth and heaven in procession.
To be seen, of course, from above; we, phantoms
of our nations, infinitesimal. I plunge my face, my beard
into the shim of it. Constellations speak to constellations,
that much is easy. Or perhaps they were meant
to channel the wind, for the wind to brush them.
Hello, I am a wounded animal and my name is pain.
The wind lathers me, scours me. This is what the wound,
cleaned, looks like, speaking to other wounds.
I have not written sufficiently of earth, and of the things
of earth. Scattered about they resemble mercy,
but they aren't that. The shell of a box turtle, whole.
The shell of a box turtle, shattered in the asphalt lane.
See: the ends of things, how we approach them.
I take the marked trail. I pass to the right of the Great
Bear Mound, I let my gaze rest upon it. I let my thought
rest upon it. Seriously, what did you think *spirit*
meant, here. It means the wind brushing this earth
and my body also. *Perforate* vs. *stipulate:* neither apply.
On the other hand, *enactment.* Of, say, the verb *to be.*
Not *to dwell.* Earth, and our participation in the works
of earth. While I was contagious, I could not thread
a needle. I know this; I tried. Needle found in a back
drawer. Thread from a sewing kit. Conceptually,
it seemed so easy: a child could do it. (I did it,
as a child.) Or, an immense and hitherto unrecognized
definition of *rest.* All that watchfulness, and other
appurtenances. You might as well deed a wheel.

I thought, I have never been less frightened in my life,
the coolness of the understory, the vagrant river
at a distance. Below, we find what things have become:
sounds and commodities, mostly. Weighed in what
balance. I press my thumb into the bole of a black gum.
For a time, and times, and half a time—the half-life
of that pressure. The verifiable miracle is that I am here.
That, and the honey locust. Together we have been saved
from something, as *for* something. Unleaving works
in both ways, in both directions. As for the soul,
we know what it does, the old hymn tells us: it stretches
its wings. That it can do this is a signature of the effable.
Meanwhile, the body. With its scoops and shovels.
Cleanses the wound, and then builds upon it.
Happily will I share this earth with you, all you creatures;
happily will I sip at the fountain of your breaths.
I widen everything until I believe in it. To walk again
where the map delayed us. Run, map, run.
And the purpose of death, disarmed. Pattern, pattern;
more remarkable the perception, the apprehension
of pattern. This, then, is a score, if you like. In the sense
that a score is what's riven inward. I try to teach
the wind a new word. That one, indispensable word:
Wound. It takes the vowel on its tongue, releases it.
I am like all the others here, built of wounds
and of wounding. The breath, at least, not a wound.
Not this time. Here, the calendar of animals, and of their
erosion. What is a year, a month, a day here: latria
of subsidence. Erosion *attends,* faithfully. This then

is the faithful wound, the breathable wound. In which I
participate, I mean my body. The animals grouped
around the creche of its becoming. Hulls of hickory nuts
left discarded on the sand of the human path. The wound
begins to finger-spell against my thigh, my chest
(for six months I packed and unpacked the gauze,
I measured, I recorded and reported my measurements).
Theology, the elaboration of primes by distinctions—
this is unlike *this.* Poor messenger, take thy frame away.
That is what this place is, or aspires to be: a subtraction
or abolition of frames. I am a clock to it, beating human
time. What if it is not about the dead (cf. Stonehenge),
but about the living. Both the human living
and the non-human living. As cosmogony, from moment
to moment. This is the world, and this is the world.
You feel your mass shifting, a bit, inside. Take a few
steps, repeat the process. O quickening face of it.
The Great Bear Mound again, replete with consequence.
The night sky between it and its brother, whom
we have drawn. *Trace,* that marvelous, magnificent
word <insert etymology here>. I will write to my friend,
it (this place) accords with Ely Cathedral. Like an Ely
set humming, waiting for us. Perhaps this is one
definition of waiting. (Perhaps *wound* is the other.)
As exercise in ecstatic waiting, then. How does it even
begin to be possible that we have not destroyed this.
Abide is not a definition of waiting, it is its pluperfect
verbal form, future-facing. We describe our penances
thus: architecture, mirrors. And *contagion*?

How other lives move through us. I know, it is painful
to think of it like this. A wind rushing towards you
and around you, and then rushing just as certainly away.

[THE HEALING LOOM]

I set to work at the healing loom I let the loom-weights fall I let the loom-weights stutter.

In the dark they spoke indifferently about suffering.

In the dark they may have been something else entirely but I was not with them in the dark.

I washed my face it was morning the flowers like flayed hands.

Whose hands I thought and who would flay them.

Instead one by one the birds arrived their eyes cracking like tiny seeds.

The healing loom had grown silent because you see I was distracted I kept prompting fate.

Fate you have forgotten your lines I hissed fate you need to talk to the director.

I grasped the shuttle in my hand it was a very good shuttle an antique you might say.

I felt it knew my hand the contours of my hand either flayed or unflayed (unflayed today).

I moistened the weft with a little milk yesterday's milk as I'd been taught.

Outside the birds were nerves in a cylinder of meat they made joyful noises.

Letters foaming at the site of the amputation like sap from a tree on fire, a cherry maybe, they spit and thrum. Whole days pass like this.

How God penetrates the baffles of matter with His non-matter is my study.

I sleep beneath the loom as it more or less precisely covers the extent of my physical body even though it is never dark here it is never quite night.

This is the pattern I intend to execute on the healing loom: *the house set on fire.*

You see the skeins of flax I've been provided with crimson citrine taupe how charming.

What I like best are the shadows they cast from their pegs on the wall.

I sit at the healing loom and contemplate these shadows for much of the day.

Day being the garment fate shed almost carelessly it seemed as it stumbled blind into form.

MOUNT GRACE PRIORY

It was not a question of not having the language for it—
having two, in fact. The walking towards it,
& then the walking away. How that felt, all the green
gathering itself to the idea of green, lingering
right at the edge of the dark, what we call the dark.
And the languages, both of them, noticing that, envying
it. From their places at the beginning & at the end.

DEPOSITION

Brownville United Methodist Church, Brownville, Nebraska

Place a charcoal sketch of a woman above the altar. She's looking up & to the left,
   beyond the frame towards precisely nothing, the nothing in the still air of the
   vacancy, the architecture.

She looks interested, but only just, or else anxious, but again, only just. She's wearing a
   loose-fitting tunic or blouse.

I photograph her, this drawing of her (possibly a reproduction). I consider the nothing,
   the vacancy, the architecture.

Being mammals, we are presumed both to breathe & to sleep.

I photograph the vessels on the back wall. I photograph the American flag, the bottle
   of hand sanitizer on the lectern.

I would never photograph another person, I mean a breathing human being, but I
   document the arrangements of absence.

I contemplate a past in which the etymological root of *chair* meant *spoken-to.*

The etymologies of the body, concealed within the body. Gracious in their con-
   cealments.

Also, the means for making fire, upon command.

To what or whom was I apprenticed, in the strictest sense: I am asking. Precision, that
   myth, versatile.

Architecture makes its single high-pitched hum, rising & falling as with the seasons
   (though not in fact with the seasons, you understand).

Test the surface for water, among other substances & features.

Ruins multiply. But the void, the vacancy is not one of them, it is present, always
   neither more nor less than fully present, it chambers as with a thought.

Thought, take me back to the brink of that ancient well, where I knelt.

Healing, what does this word even mean?

It means adjusting to new sounds, & to the penetration of the body by new sounds,
   in new ways.

It means a recovery of the faculty of joy.

28

I follow the gaze of the drawn or painted woman who is not Christ, up & out of the frame.

The economy edges towards me. I recognize it by its peculiar odor, speculative in the root sense (that is, with the glint of a mirror where an ethics should be).

My lost organs shout in triumph, in some other place or dimension. I don't hear them. But it is a biblical shout, somehow I understand. They have forded the perilous current.

I try kneeling here, I try my kneeling knee. It is a new pain to me. I spend some time with it, this new pain.

Pain, an absence masquerading as a presence, as the surgeon taught me.

Or, he added, it can derive from presence, a malign presence. (Pursue then the difference between absence & presence.)

I listen to the casual photosynthesis of ancient beings, through the thick glass.

Once I lit the tapers for the Yule feast. I was a child then, & whole.

We age into our necessities, which consume us. Moving from museum to museum, I found myself battling a medical feeling, a *déjà vu*.

Yes to the photograph, yes to the vintage implements on display in the refurbished kitchen, yes to the wax lemon slices.

I thought, distinctly, What would happen if I fell, now, insensible, to the floor? From any cause?

Ahead of me one docent & then another, praising the nation & its residue.

Everybody wants to arrive just in time for the holidays, the gatherings of the appetite to which we'd apprenticed ourselves & our children. Everybody wants an autograph.

Here, in this place, the last place of active worship in this locale (this place), used for worship—by myself, now.

As custom bade. As mercy required, that is, demanded. In time of plague.

I let them vote, my miscast organs. For surely they are citizens.

The woman in the drawing looks up & out of the frame. Perhaps there is a cruelty in
  her expression, a gentle cruelty, a cruel gentleness.

Once again I am matter in the church of matter. I run my fingers along the gilt edges.

My breath, extraordinary. My sleep likewise.

Or perhaps, having seen it, the object of her desire, she is about to turn, run towards it,
  to it. (If not imprisoned by the frame.)

I gather light, bushel upon bushel, from the specters of the orchards. I am fat with
  light.

Other beings & objects do respond to touch, if infinitesimally. I bore a flame into the
  furnished world.

Or perhaps it is not a woman at all, but a young Christ, an adolescent or pre-adoles-
  cent Christ. I mean, a representation.

At that age what might have caught His attention (I wonder). Perhaps a dove, perhaps
  a flock of doves. They remind Him of something.

Perhaps the sounds of children (other children) playing in the street.

In the rear of the church, a large Bible, the pages bent back so that viewed upright &
  from the side, the image of a cross presents.

I photograph it—twice, as if both before & after some great accident.

Place being of course a gospel category, an epistemology, a hermeneutics. It practices
  upon my body, as upon an instrument.

This is the sound place makes practicing upon my body. This is a chrysanthemum, this
  is a knife.

Deixis, the point gesturing towards the line, the line gesturing towards the plane. The
  god in that.

I am the ruin the past has made, & then discarded. With each breath I participate in
  my abandonment.

The forfeit of objects, such happy mischance. Let's stage a nation there.

Last of the loosestrife fading now in the hedgerows, what new epic have I squandered.

Bleed properly, I misread. Breathe properly (o my chevalier).

The image, which has so little time. How the light plays against it.

I touch my own face, which is, of course, forbidden now. I step again into the place I
    have never been & watch it falling there, addressed so prominently.

FOUNTAINS ABBEY, PENTECOST

Let's be quick to claim. Gnaw gnaw like an orchard
in the grip of an August thirst. What knowledge
took us this far, towards the intromission of tenancy.
It clings to me like a crown. A legible devotion,
the angles that bring into focus all our truest blames.
You may run your hand over them if you like.
Consider the lips of animals as one more check
signed by God, one more IOU. I present their wars
to the assembly which falls silent for a brief period
because we have so many wars, why not feast.
Early fruit of the season split and roasting on a fire
the world obscures with its ragged hem.
Strong muscles of the throat meant for wings
goes one argument, not necessarily mine but how
the scars constrict when paraphrased, by oil or wine.
This all takes some time as I'm sure you know.
I place my rage in my bag. It is not what you think.
Writing on the nature of friendship Aelred
fell deep into the archaic crush of prescriptive
fear. Of course he was drawing from nature, what
else is there to draw from, mixed pigments sweating
in their wooden bowls. Soon it will be possible
to take the life of a woman or man you've never
seen, a form of taxidermy that relies upon the soul
as its armature, then clothes it. As with gratitude.
Glass eyes where the actual eyes had been.
It's hard to remember isn't it glass as something
new, glass as one substitute for the natural tendency
to shine a bright light, or turn away. Be sure
to record all the shadows cast by the feast, that is,

by the assembly when it settles into the posture
of appetite. Sketch every one. In the meantime
practice the management of water, as of fire.
The difference is, one can fall into water
(though of course one can also fall into fire).
Ropes tied around the perimeter to prevent any
such accident. But they are flammable too in turn.
And soluble, should they remain submerged.
I'm talking about ropes *then.* Ropes now
are made from synthetics that will last forever.
Watch for them in paintings by the Renaissance
masters, Bartolomé Bermejo perhaps, how
he manages to burn without painting actual fire
which is also something ropes can do
when they run too fast through your hands.
Or paintings of ropes through paintings of hands,
little physics experiments. It had been Lent
but that was some time ago, a spurned archive.
Little moan, disavow thirst's hollow fingers,
a foaming thread. And I said *lustral unmeasured*
skeins, or so the chronicle insists. It is possible.
I do not recall the moment clearly. It is alleged
the Victorian children's author Anne Jane Cupples
once corresponded with Darwin about a possible
position for her husband, and later Darwin
"corresponded with her about her observations
of emotions in dogs." This seems a fair trade.
There are so many more forms knowledge can take
than fire, a problem photosynthesis tries to solve.
We watch it submerging the orchard.

We watch it strip thorns from the raspberry canes.
Not like in the story where the dead man
remains dead, not like that at all. Although
that is a story each of us knows by heart, indeed
carries with us *in* each heart. That little parable
of where the blood flowed and where we caught it
in our various receptacles of glass, stone, wood.
This is text, it could just as well have been blade
flying through theories of parthenogenesis.
I will now stoop to sweep up the dead flies
that have collected in the forecourt. Nothing else.

CREATION MYTH SUITE

(1)

The deer do not know
the earth is round.
Somehow
they bear their young
anyway, in Vermeer's
blond glow.
By the lake I sank
to my damaged knees,
not having met
any citizen of memory.
The lepers drifted
westward, bleary
in their treaty-dances,
their prophet's
muscle. In this posture
the revolution
began, spinning lazily
backwards
into presidencies,
lush and unrestrained.

(2)

I can write no more
about bread
than about tin,
each of which
the sunrise presents

to me in turn:
Tin or bread, bread
or tin.
I once held a gun
while cancer
rucked my blood's
cast-iron
vein. I convoked
a parliament
of bridges,
to which I pled
my scabbed kinship.
Bread or tin, tin
or bread
they chanted
until, at length, I
left that island.
Nothing burned
more brightly than
the oldest
ladder, its rungs
silver with
splinters. *Are you*
not astonished,
the sunrise
demands, swigging
its chalky nectar.
I am a war
is what I tell it,
then. It nods, it

has read the book,
it can see
time's other motion.

(3)
I painted my bed
with pomegranates
& turtledoves:
I wanted
to worship there,
in the crutch
or crux of memory.
For six nights
I set the cut
flowers of dusk
in a vase
next to my bed,
let them sing
their silent hymns.
I hid my garments
from my
old man's beard,
blessed them
on their journeys
reckoned according
to the algorithms
of dry planets.
Instead I hemmed

the lashes of
love's stone lyre,
its dense &
superscripted vowel.
Dawn met me
in bitter knots,
knocked
a continent
from my right hand.

(4)

Here I am, with my pulse
of thorns.
My limbs are churches
at which my navel
worships.
They ascend & descend
like frontiers,
bleak about their frayed
edges. I have
stopped all the clocks
again, so that
we can weigh the yews
without further
interruption. Be a throne,
my physicians insist;

be a thirsty
spar. The greatest
honey sheathes
both our armies, Master.

(5)

At my summons
a lamp
left its burden
along the old road.
It brought
bells with it.
I traded the bells
for a city.
I slept inside
night's
insomniac eye.
May I go then
the lamp inquired.
We paused
at the edge
of the orchard
my father planted,
pruning hooks
glinting
in both our exiles.

(6)

Let the thirsty wedding
launder
our venous baptisms,
let them dwindle
in the city of shepherds
where no shepherds
ever come. I lay
my ash against a myth
& recite
the catechism of pollen.
My lungs are the dawn
no sun
will ever witness,
a helm of trembling
erasures. Like breath
they fragment
as they char
into vows: vows, &
all their lucid shadows.

ACADIA WINTER POEM

Mount Desert

Go, said the solstice, or my memory of the solstice. So I went.
Waves of iron lashed a coast made of rope.
You will not have to count things anymore. You will leave the flag
in its tri-fold upon the dark
mantelpiece, showing only the blue & six white stars.
I smelt smoke, or oil burning. (And people asked,

how did your study of history inform your labors.) Where stones
on the shore cradled other stones:
here, now. There is the green that invites winter in, & the green
that regards winter as both its nest & its scar.
What is difficult is to know how to wait for the invitation:
should you spend the time

(for instance) in a lab, or washing clothes on the clean rocks.
I study the lichen with my pitched voice: is it a prison, or a comity.
In any event, ice, the ice in the eyes of the servitor,
the land's chirp & gurgle. Let's wait here,
no, here, where the hunter reckons his kill. The hunter, too, invited.
His dogs are small gods fallen into a tight dream.

The bridge clasps the scroll of the mountain's flank like a knife
just before the cut. Remember the lovers, their breaths
a mist obscuring the bright canvas.
Mathematics permits this much, & more. Later, I discuss
with my brother, weary from two days of laying pipe,
the age-old question of how much a spiritual man should laugh,

whether in smiling show his teeth. My brother
is an animal rising from the earth at dusk. Our God, likewise.
What makes all this possible
is a shadow the birds flee, in quick strikes: tree to tree
to tree. I had replaced my voice with something permanent,
a ghost perhaps, the sound

not of berries ripening but of berries having ripened
a season ago. I hold the torch of my shin to it, watch it flare, record
the result with my good hand in the red notebook
where the moon-shaped animals gather, kneel, & drink.
Worshipers pressed into the great announcement, swift plunges
into the matte orchard with its sweet,

dark fruit. You make the year strange, with your prayers & shadows.
You are the story of the wounded sentinel
who would not leave his post, not for all the Bibles washed
up against the stones of this wracked strand. I swathe the lintel
with your gauze of gold. My breath must suffice,
for all of us. I scatter it like ash or spawn. I was your guest,

I was your vendor of milk, it was I who told you the legend of winter
as I passed. The deep brass bell of darkness
ringing against both plow & net. A raptor shook me
from the dim musk of my enemy. I held nothing, then. I listened
to the empire ripen, a Babylon in its green tent. To sing
or to make war together. I can hear the chimes from this place

called *here*. A place electricity has not known,
nor any ellipsis. Set like a maul on a stump, or like a censer
washed, dried, laid carefully in a cabinet
to which only a priest holds the key. The island raises its candle
into the myrrh of winter. Error commences in just this way,
without benefit of blame. We straddle these worlds. Apotropaic

burn marks on the timbers of our ancient house
in the court of which we, as children, gladly spun. Now the thieves
begin to sing. They are thirsty. It is hard work, thievery.
Squirrels & jays call after us, angrily. They live on the island.
Their tiny bones are the ground we walk on.
It takes a tremendous effort to lift a season from the water—

there, its back, black with streaming. It has too many arms,
that's right. Or you have too few. You, ash from a fire,
never serious. What can you mend with fire, what can you mend
with bone. The seasons lurch away from you,
the moment that is you. High above Monument Cove
I listen to the clack of stone washing other stones. Other people

are simply unfathomable: the woman, for instance, sitting alone
on an outcrop of pink granite
a quarter mile to the north. I am listening to stones
but it's her I see, knees drawn up beneath her chin, face tilted
just a bit high, as if she's thinking,
reconsidering. My eye snagged on what turned out

to be a turquoise thread wrapped tightly around
a bit of bistered vegetation, old flower-head caught out by frost.
For a moment the sea stopped playing the king
in some winter play.
It was cold; I pulled my face more tightly about my skull.
Winter palette: grays, greens, the dead blues

of deep chill, striations in pegmatite. To fall, there, to one knee,
there, in that place, at the eye's behest:
was not prayer. Was neither cry nor accident. Was merely
something the mouth knows, when it opens to breathe,
when one is otherwise sleeping
in the night. *Winter palette*, what the breath wakes from stone:

basalt, granite. Salt. Green, the greens,
all the greens—you gather them in the muscles of your eye.
You tell them apart. You tell them: apart from the sea, abiding.
The smallest, the gray-green of that tiny lichen, there—
listens, seems to nod. You put your brush
away, you who came here. You stow the flag inside the star.

SAINT SAUVEUR

Mount Desert

Am I music? is what
   the water asks. (It isn't.)

I spend some time
with lichen
encased beneath a sheath
  of transparent ice.

I wait
for the years
  to drop away from me.
(They don't.)

Everything listens
a little,

including the past (what
  we think of as the past,
    which is a ghost).

This is the non-sound
of everything
listening.

It's what poetry aspires to.

Hush now,
   children I never had.
   Let water
comb the ghosts away.

You can't
not judge me anymore.

BELL BUOY, OTTER CLIFFS

Acadia National Park

And the spirit says, *Wake.*

And the birches say,
Do you want to talk about this no I don't want to talk about this okay okay then
what do you want to talk about I don't want to talk at all then what do you want
to do if not talk really we must do something—

etc. etc.
b/c birches, the social tree.

Because
the soul is magnetic, meaning
it contains iron.

This much is certain. Not,
what is the manner
of your choosing.

Noon. I hoard my shadow.

All things
end here, is what the soul,
waking, says.

It is mistaken.
The spirit says, *Try again.*

CONTEMPLATING THE PIPPA BLACKALL MILLENNIUM WINDOW AT ALPHETON CHURCH, ST. PADARN'S DAY 2021

West Suffolk

You put your sheaves away. (I put my sheaves away.) Memory
strikes its toned bell. I am alive with breath here, & with
something much larger, that is like breath, but not breath.
Light roots in it, by way of glass. Look (I am looking), the light
streaming through the earth tones, Suffolk light, late afternoon
April light. It's true, I walked through hail to get here. Festive,

the hail striking the ancient hawthorn hedge, which is dying
in patches, its great vertebrae. Together we rose over the crest
of the ridge. I am neither more nor less than this, these works,
this record. What would you work in glass if you could,
is one question faith asks, mostly at night. The brilliant lapis
not of Mary (though her niche survives) but of the farm truck

speeding north. Suffolk blues, Suffolk browns, Suffolk grays.
The root, its alchemical striving: it wants to reach the depths,
the depths are its dream, its consummation. *Come unto me*
read the words burned into the porch beam, they can't
stop saying this, proclaiming. Kerygma, an earthen jar—
filled with water, or honey, or oil. Or, empty. I let the light

flood into me, through the image of Christ. Now the saints
are conversing, they are in deep & earnest conversation,
they have perhaps brought a gift. One looks like he is having
doubts, the other as if he, sympathetic, is comforting him,
trying to comfort him, to reassure. Elsewhere a woman bends
to her needlework in the inbled light. She, too, a record,

making a record. Twin heads of wheat riding the high wind,
they make a little monastery for the hands to go to sleep in.
Sheaves, the standing shocks, use them as keys. The sheep
in their hurdle pen, the single horse. The crowns rest on them.
Because it is in the nature of crowns, to rest. See the surface
to which the arrows were drawn, breeding things.

Let it be a king if it must (if you must). I am empty of hymns
at this time. I hold the water to its rhythm, etched in glass.
Carry a child (or a sheep, it's difficult to say, through
centuries of time's disfigurement, the flaking of the plaster)
across the Kedron that remedies this, all of this, that promises
healing. For we shall all be changed. You, as well as I,

vagrant in the light slipping to the west. (*Faithless,*
I was going to add, but of course light is faithless.) This bit
of space snipped from other space, from the rich fields
arising. It's certainly possible to tell a story through tracks
left in cloth, ancient authorities agree. The dimming
reaches me, feels me with its blind hand, remembers, passes

on. I had in fact prepared a song, laid it bare or bound it
with cords, I brought it with me, across the brook, across
these gentle acres. But it recognized some other master (song,
so fickle). Perhaps this is the right place to ask again
what *emblem* means, what light wakes from it
(or the dark) (for we wake both in the light & in the dark).

The image of belief believing, so bright! It shares itself.
This is its cursive script genuflecting. This is me completing
the action of the body in a strange place, a place to which
I am a stranger. I have not been abandoned, all this is entirely
outside & beyond the economy of abandonment. Barley
making its drowsing way to market, how many centuries now,

its joyful lapse. In this place Christ is a young farmer
in working clothes, a bit distracted perhaps, it's the land
He recognizes, sheaves within sheaves, all those minuscule
deaths. Glass, the breakable praise. In the hall of plenty
we refreshed & were refreshed, we comforted with what
comfort we framed within ourselves. We learned our letters,

one by one. Because it is, once again, in the nature of crowns—
to rest. Not to rise, though the ancient glass in the south-
facing canopies beckons, reassembled, a glossolalia. Each
pane a tongue. Sheets of tongues, descending. Tongues
fixed in iron & to other tongues, for the light to pass through.
Which is what the light does best, its generous paraphrase.

THE HOLY SPIRIT AS A VOWEL
IN EARLY SNOW (II)

1.

Blur of unlikeness, wake in me.

Wake me, then teach me.

I bled winter from my happiness,
I brushed it
from my collar & my sleeve.

Thus I was discovered, a wind.

2.

A traveler's psalm. Mark me.

Picture this: my eyes
walking towards the distant sun.

The sheep lie down
in the green
lungs of their pastures, at rest.

3.

Bitterness, an ark
crowded with students. *Marry me*
is their signature call.

4.

The hero as direct object:
aren't we
tired of this, & so much more.

Christ
of the preposition,
skimming the frozen waters:

5.

All that is not
& could never be a parable.

TO A SHELF FUNGUS IN ACADIA NATIONAL PARK

Fomitopsis pinicola

Hail, true body.
You are not an echo,
deep in the death-
wood you exalt
your quiet syntheses.
You are not a mirror,
not a fish or a flash.
Toys haunt you,
or flee from you,
the bit of escaped gas
that warns the patrons
of the all-night laundry
to slip, one by one,
into the unlit street.
I would sing to you
but singing is wrong,
sometimes—and you
need no lullaby.
You have painted
your nails
the vivid red
chromium dreams
of, when chromium
dreams. It would be
unlike you to pretend
to decoration, being,
as you are, a spirit
encased in a block
of jagged fir.

The ruins of a forest
were the first
cinema, surely.
You are the light
that shines demurely
through the vintage
celluloid.
On the far wall
my image shifts,
shudders, drops.
You are the acoustic
solved for X. The salt
does not much
bother you, or flames
in parliaments.
I could place a stone,
a very small stone,
in your hair, your
outstretched hand.
I don't. You are not
the recipient
of human passions,
though your praise
ascends in choirs.
It's as if
you've woken
a new breath, not
from the infant body
but from that other,

that stopped clock,
dismissed
from the infirmary.
Truly
magi read in you
a parable of stars,
& of the destruction
of stars. I wander
through your house
like the stranger
that I am,
here, & you let me.
Algae tents
along your lower
belvederes, &
you let it. You open
the door to no
church, because it is
the church of no
you occupy
so fully. And isn't it
fitting, to occupy
a church so fully.
You ring no bells.
You light no censer.
If I pressed my ear
to the nave of you,
what would I hear?
My own heart

beating rapidly,
suspended
within July's
chronic inflammation.
And you have
children I will never
see, spectral bailiffs.
Is it possible
that your experience
is a form of joy?
Or a word for joy,
in an unspeakable
tongue. Forest
of lapsed breads
entindered,
your skete.
You gentle awning.

AT THE GEORGE CALEB BINGHAM HOUSE, ARROW ROCK, MISSOURI

You could say: this is where a people's art began.
Malaria; cicada whine. You could dress yourself up
in your wounds. You may walk in the center
of the road, as far as you like. Vanity,
to center the composition just so. You smile into it.
You wait for it to ask you a question. You could say:
the roughed-in portrait on the easel is a prop,
a mere prop. Beside the basket of vintage needlework,
pincushions, pins & needles rusted into the gay fibers.
If you are unable to walk then you might limp.
The question turns beneath your hand. It turns but it
does not break, & here you are. You could say:
marry me, pigments sprung from lead, from lapis,
from madder (a mere prop). All the blind heroes
from the past are clapping. The city is clapping, Zion
if you like. Whisper your signature into the variation:
the new bottoms through which the river once ran.
It is easy to imagine hunters here, so why not do it:
hunters. Cracks varnished over, you can see them
in this late light. The gardeners arrive & then withdraw.
You could say art sent them. You could say art
slew them. You could pioneer the use of red
underpainting, to confer a lifelike blush to human
figures, to a young nation. Overspreading
older nations, yes, the clamor sealed within the image.
You are astonishingly not alone, is the message
daybreak broke against the thighbone of a saint.
What if you pierce it. What if you make a musical

instrument of it. What then would you have waited for,
yes, I (is it time for the "I") am asking you.
Who have glimpsed this world, & possibly others.
Speak with the thread in your hands. Cicada whine
upthrust from the depths, into the plane of desire
which is to say, of representation. You, you, you,
eyes shut, eyes wide, make your decision, this stroke
versus that stroke, assisted by the glistening hairs
of an animal, some former animal. The image *alive*
alive-o as it must be. Here is the body of a pelican
stretched on a strand, here is the body of a crow
stretched on a wooden table, here is a marmot, here
is a mink (with a human hand showing, bottom left,
as if reaching for it or perhaps as if withdrawing).
You may think of the heaven of images, if there is one—
you may think there is one. An infinite plane
of perfect representations. And every fourteen years,
or every seventeen, that desperate clawing up
through the surface, that seeking. The slit
harvested just so. Uninvented because it is closed,
as all conquest is closed. Now the docent has
returned to lock the room back up, & you thank her.

TARRY

Big Spring, Arrow Rock, Missouri

The body records its absences. Water, you take water
into it—as presence, as absence, deep into the archive
of water you throw your mask. Also, your other mask.
We, being matter, are negotiated. I had not thought
to be angry, as such. But rage flexes its majestic undoing,
its sustaining negation. The reparations the body seeks
rest in time. Perhaps they *are* time. I am not insensible
to the sounds water makes flowing. Or not flowing.
Tune thy instrument, o Captor. This is the present.
I decline in it like a verb from some unknown tongue.
I knelt at the octagonal well-cap—no. Nothing
like that, not here. In this place of coming & becoming.
What did the life say to the light, runs a joke.
My blood, also running, as if in jest. I admired it
at the blurred edges. I am not unhappy, or not rigorously
so. I retain my privacies. The trees here, strange to me,
extruded. A man measures himself against such divers
entities. It is early (for me). Low musky trill of some
fledged form. As if ancient, as if an intelligence placed
its thumb just there, in morning mist. I, too, am broken
into majesties: rage; blood; lead. Cold-flow
of the soundscape around me, what chain have I forged,
this terrible vagrancy. I score it for judgment,
among the arteries my mouth has known. A new breeze
dries the sweat against my cheek, I lift my hand to it
(breeze; sweat; cheek) as if casting myself in some drama.
I swing back the great bronze gate. *Tarry,* what is it,
what can it be *made* of. For surely it is constructed,
like a house, amidst this oxygen. We can step

inside & out again, tourists. Or, we can dwell. That verb,
to dwell—it hangs from the line, it flaps in the breeze,
it is not a cage because look, the cage is right here.
You may view it through polarized glass. You
may touch it (if you believe in the grammar of matter).
Make the scar tremble, yes, that's it. A small seed blows
or falls into the crook of the book, armored. Some feasts
are very small, we walk right past them, as if the moon
weren't real in daytime. It is real. In the day.
There, behind where the cage last stood, & rising.
Waters respond to it, we know this. I have been deceived
but not by matter, never. Not by the hands of princesses
or kings. I washed myself & laced myself into
a thought, a stance. Betook myself to an ancient place.
Refused memory, aside from language (itself a trace).
And now the miniature appeals, each from its petitioner.
It is too early for wonder but not too early for prayer.
—There. As cage this prayer. Touch it or else don't,
the day says, avid & prinked. There's no new distance
here. I rub my thought against it, as against the cries
from the forest which is, I am told, new in the scheme
of all things, that is, of men. A locust leaf lodges
in my beard. I was much smaller than this, I suspect,
when I had cancer, when I gnawed the red latch.
White white white of the non-sky with a moon
superimposed. These waters, unlocking for it. Both
those in my body & those at my side, those that still
bear within them the hair & spoor of the strangers' dogs,
splashing freely in the moment just before my arrival.

AND THE STONESQUARERS
(1 Kings 5:18)

Arrow Rock Christian Church, Arrow Rock, Missouri

Faith vacates, leaves no forwarding address.
           We store things in the emptied nave:
boxes of fabric, folding tables & chairs, weddings
     when the occasion calls for them.
                    Most occasions call for vacancy.
I mean minute by minute, hour by hour, day by day.
The dust settles, prodded by the infinitesimal
           shaft of air
              cast by a wasp that has found its way
in, its brief & manic flight.
           Let the wasp wake the dust, is one option.
Wait for the wasp to become dust, is another.
     Time, a gift towards which
           planets hurl themselves, streaming
              silent compensations. We can perhaps
still write to faith, general delivery.
   Here in faith's house John Cage's drone—
                    "as slow as possible"—
seems very far away, & it is.
A recent chord change made the major dailies.
I shared it, the news, with others, two or three friends.
   This room scored for rain, passing cars, dust,
                    & breath. My breath.
The scratching of my pen, this pen.
   Orator, our compensation, what has become of it.

You must speak clearly now.

     You may clutch or rend your garments.

       Strike low against the worn bell's absence
then list again, lean into

   matter playing matter as in some village play.
One by one the strings relinquished,

                  falling back

         into the self that hovers

     at the dim edge of precision.
The hole in the ceiling, the scuffed hardwood floor

    where the stove once stood, for winter worship.
The wasp at the rolled pane, its insistence

     (the wasp's, not the pane's)

        beginning to flag. Should I go to it
as I would to a child wounded, or dying. Should I

    comfort it. Lie down within the waking gap,
that aperture—

   & see, I do, I am alone here,

    a dust among dusts. The organ case is locked.
A few hymnals remain stacked in a corner pew.

   There is a piano, I press a key—

      middle C—test my voice against it.

         Shocked! the dust protests:
that's it, I have shocked the dust. It quiets.

   My own organs quiet, both the present

           & the absent.
Of the latter I dream, from time to time.

"Medical waste" the head nurse referred to them
but why not be creative, why not
        call them "garden of hidden stones."
Why not call them "spy-holes of enough."
                              It is sufficient,
    the pair of vows,
        one kept, the other broken: my life
            borne before the jeweled altars.
Here, the dais. Here, the lectern, carved
from chunky poplar stained to resemble oak.
                It draws a world to it
      & names that "hunger"—not *my* hunger—
                    it confesses nothing
& in thus not-confessing it abides.
    It is a remnant of a living thing, so easy
                   to forget this, the pews,
the planked floors, the organ case (locked),
    all fossil life.
Fire frees everything from the sheer pretension
                of believing one has a soul.
The sound of fire has a depth,
   how might one measure it? Against
       this non-silence, this wasp-silence, the glass
        silent (but remember: cold-flow),
   the silence of the wood's slumber or slow decay.
The light, arguably, more silent.

I raise & then lower my hand
            as if I had a question. This is system,
the wood, the glass, the iron nails & fixtures
        bound together
                just so. Raw soul, what the saints
are or were served on chipped plates.
    Pain is a banquet, evidently
                        we are meant to sate ourselves.
But back to the depth of the sound of flames,
    how could we measure that?
                I look closer, I examine the detail,
a spray of leaves carved into the organ case,
            scars carved into the back of my left hand.
I meant them for music,
    I confess: one, two, three, four, five lines.
                        I open a hymnal at random,
"My Anchor Holds" in all its 19th-century
        piety, sung here I'm certain, someone's favorite.
For I know wildly. Soul griefs like billows.
        Don't you want to
    take some photographs, the docent had asked,
but I said no, I was done with photographs.
Faith photographs a leg, a bluff,
            stray hair left on a barber's dirty tiled floor.
Or, faith is a rib
    you can play—anyone can play—
        as a musical instrument, G#, B, D#,
                                minor triad
the wasp, wherever it is, must register.

Earlier my hands were shaking but not now.
    I consider the lilies, rather doubtful anchors.
I ask for more raw soul,
    perhaps with a sprinkle of vinegar.
Are condiments permitted, at the banquet of pain?
But let the makers come, let them occupy,
        what have we
                to fear, or to lose. (I am no longer
                        certain of the difference.)
I press one hand to the small of my back,
    that useless cupping, I wash my hand
            in that emptiness. I part my lips, for now
a motion that brings no pain
    & makes the slightest
                    sound, how should I score it, the two
lightly-moistened labial ridges tensing,
        then separating.
                    I blow the citadel right through it,
where I can see it, momentarily (for it is autumn).
    Such music I once made with this, my body.
I climbed the low wall to retrieve
                —what? I can't remember, only the feel
of the wet, cold, crumbling mortar
    beneath my palms, & the grip of them,
                        then the relinquishment.

The metric blind to its own fulfillment
which recurs both in & outside time
    & for which I have tarried,
here, though smaller now & facing toward the story
    my brother told me, the flashing wound
                that draws everything to itself
& in which the fire balloons rise, in twos & threes,
faint luffing sound each makes as it drifts
    vaguely in the direction
        of the barn, the field, & then the forest
    I recognize only from the postcards
pinned to the felt board on the museum's far wall.

GRIEVANCE

Arrow Rock Christian Church, Arrow Rock, Missouri

First, we will attempt to present it in writing, then in speech.
This failing, we will try song, instrumental music,
& then the textile arts. I abandoned the metric
once it had cooled, having wrapped it in red thread
so that the soldiers, patrolling the perimeter, would spot it
more readily. We move out from things,
things move out from us. We invented the narrow gap
through which God shines nightly, as billed. Consolation,
what matches it, I mean through whom or what
is one commensurate. I think of the times I have been
shot (zero), the times I have been shot at (zero),
the times a gun has been leveled at me, loaded, safety off
(twice, to my knowledge). I will show this to the sleepers
lowered in heart to the drinking vessel of unknown origin
left by the ancient well. Thirst, sleep, drink, wake
(is one definition, of love I suspect). It is so heavy,
& to withdraw it from its niche requires not only strength
but also poise, the body's core disposed just so.
I write this as though I had once killed another man,
although I haven't. Waxed threads flaring as we cast them
into the flames, who needs them anymore?
What else haven't I wrapped my arms around.
I place my hand on a carving of some stylized floral spray
on the side of the organ case. It is low & so I conclude
the last person to do this was probably
a child. I press my palm against a pew as if testing it
for fever. Never open a pew if the pew is hot to the touch.

This pew is cold, smooth & cold & my thought chisels
through it, to the void on the other side where the wiring,
provisional, awaits trained hands. My attention is a spool,
wooden, flecked with spit & blood & I
wind my sensory data around it. *Within the wilderness*
a rest. And catch a gleam of glory bright. Oh Protestantism,
you have never known me, only my shadow at morning
& dusk. You say I see the animals in their burrows
but you lie, you lie, the structures of empathy are bent &
no longer conduct heat, light, or even electricity
as they were designed to do. Once, I jammed a stick
between the jaws of an epileptic girl seizing on the library
steps, I didn't know her, it was summer, I was walking
& saw her fall, convulse. When the police arrived
I slipped away. I took refuge in the high places.
I was not present at the unveiling. The light is wrong
for this, my father said, frowning, leaning close to where
the tool should fit, to do its work. I said nothing
to the double rainbow arcing over the supermarket
parking lot. Discover—have you any right.
You run your lines again, forward & then backward,
you test the back of your tongue against the backs
of your teeth. *Yes, I do. No, I will not.* Everything
collects the brightness & hoards it, as if the past were real.
It isn't, except in vows, & in the breaking of vows.
The delay in representation is slight, a simple offset
by which the celebrants assert their probity.

Politics, what can be said of politics, it's the frayed hem
of the garment we wear, we can't take it off.
Here, a needle. Here, a lit match. *Mean everything,*
the elderly priest told me, while rubbing
the stump of his left arm with his intact right arm
& hand. & of course without a body it's true, I could
never have traced these figures in the millennial dust.

I AM THE VINE

Arrow Rock Christian Church, Arrow Rock, Missouri

I am the vine, said the vine
& traced an image of itself
across the sun's matte hook.
It was at this point I noticed
the holes in the glass.
Tiny, round, with circular divots
chipped away around them,
from the impact.
Four in one window, one each
in two others. This glass is old,
thick, it did not shatter.
As if someone had shot
at the church with buckshot
or BB's. More likely BB's.
Someone has shot at this church.
Why would anyone shoot
at an abandoned church,
is a question. In use
1872 to 1951, a decent life
for a woman or a man,
less impressive
for a house of worship.
I am the vine, said the vine,
& you, my vinedressers,
have forsaken me. You have all
gone away. They shot
from the west, the damage
is in the western windows, not
the eastern. Does this mean

anything? I am the vine, & you
are the architects of damage
in your costumes
of corduroy & silk.
You have abandoned me,
my carved image in the detail
of what would,
in some other time
or place, have been the chancel
arch. There is no chancel,
only the nave
in the prevailing Protestant
fashion: a large box
into which we have placed
if not faith, then
the residue of faith.
I am the vine, said the vine,
& you are my abandoners.
In this county alone fifteen men
& women were born
& died exactly when you did,
here. I will name them:
John E. Alpers & Ivan L. Aulgur.
Elizabeth Jane Dye, Marie E.
Fisher, William Rickney Hanks.
Elizabeth Mary Heilman.
Ulysses Solomon Neff, Alonzo
Earl O'Dell, Emelie W. Pragman.
Lena Rehkop, Milton Hume

Smith. Samuel E. VanBuskirk.
Annie S. Wellner, Laurence
Henry Winslow, Thomas Woods.
These were women & men,
they placed their hands
at some time or another
(many times) against wooden
planks, they sampled majesty.
Some handled guns.
Shall we gather by the river
that has moved over a mile
to the east, as if in flight
from us. I walk there in the rain
past the sloughs, the chutes,
the willows & poplars
with their precarious hold
on precarious ground.
I am the vine, I repeat
to the vines, the Virginia creeper
& poison ivy, the wild grape.
You have abandoned me,
I repeat to the river, when
I reach it, where it is for now.

TO EACH LIGHT OF WHICH I AM A BROTHER

Brown Lodge No. 22, A.F. & A.M., Arrow Rock, Missouri

In the disused lodge hall I am listening for the sound of brightness, which has breadth.
      Not the sound of fire, which has depth.

The candidates line up, as if for inspection.

Even in a small house objects (mostly small objects) may be hidden.

Light reaches through to where the gavels once lay. Is brightness, then, a pedestal, were
      we to approach it.

Miltonic light, not bright exactly, but in conversation with brightness. It can pierce
      milk, assert ancient authorities.

Peephole with its handmade cover like a raindrop, a drop of milk, mercury, or blood.
      At certain times one would swing the cover wide & view the other. Admit or
      deny.

Brightness, not the same as whiteness though often mistaken for it in two-dimension-
      al representations.

The sound the gavels made, wood against wood, word against word.

I recognize fire by the absence of fire, & the depths from which that absence emerges.

House by house, tales of houses being moved, by mule team, on log rollers. Everything
      here is both palimpsest & tabernacle.

The material is the wholly necessary part, where both inception & reception of sound
      are concerned.

I sat quite still & let my blood work it out for me.

If I had a prism in this place, what would I see (through it) (or, otherwise). The worn
      wood, a fossil, photosynthetic reach locked into its last amplitude.

To purify the sounds, to wash them clean—how?

I make no mistakes. Or, the mistakes I make become my cisterns, my lovers, split mi-
      gration around which the bright ships canter.

Push back the latch & search the depths. (We say "depths," plural—why?)

Electricity, neither brightness nor fire, its surface hum: we tolerate it, & much more.

I listen for measure, for the instruments of measure. *Topolithic,* a word I absorbed
      without being subject to what we call pain, also *grammetry.*

Rolled glass of the old windows seeking the center but so slowly. Brightness in its many
    modulations: can't be handled.

At this point a prayer may be offered (among the many desolations already mentioned,
    for instance children, my own or others').

I take a deep breath, sound a B-flat, more or less. It leaps the baffles matter presents, it
    magnifies.

In the rear of the derelict dwelling a scrap of sheet music was found: a hymn I knew.
    Scored for voice, for neither fire nor brightness, that is, for the human.

The vitrine, which promises both attention & safety, falsely. I breathe on it, I bend
    closer.

Shout at the fire if you like.

Friendship, association, these common aims, you must make something of something,
    as out of nothing.

I rest my living body on the bodies of others.

Does *rest* make a sound, & if so, how can we hear it, what prosthetic do we use. I see
    you with my hearing, as upon a narrow ladder.

Value, a test.

Comfort ye, my people (says your God). Not a ladder, but a filter. Not a rudder, but a
    wine. Inheritance, subject to arbors.

Brightness, which knows time as periodicity & decay, two vagrant nodes.

Everything here could be so rapidly returned to oxygen & carbon. & yet, for a little
    while—

I strengthen my aloneness in the midst of the fast. I prepare my rituals, this & divers
    others.

This one, though. You blow into it, as if it contained a single burning taper. You mea-
    sure yourself against precisely this.

All the gavels have been broken, surely: at any rate they are no longer here.

And the wasps' nest: what does it do? Effloresce? Genuflect?

You see me, but do you recognize me (is a question). The altars constructed of symbols
        & flesh, as per tradition. You offer—what?
Not forgetting the impact of a series of disastrous floods & fires, nor the violence man
        does to man. Empathy, that outlier, elliptical.
I imagine—no, it is not the time for imagining.
Address your elders thus, as you have been instructed.
Now the brightness in its bathing-state stays, remands itself. It has, in truth, known
        fire, & fire's hollow drum.
The death to which I'm promised, does it know me here (I slide the peephole cover
        back into place).
Matter is sonant; spirit is—something else. Something full, towards which the risks
        align. It receives matter cordially: *Yes. You are welcome.*

IN THE EPOCH OF BRONZE

We make the time pass.

See, the devices
laid out on the long tables,
such ingenuity.

This is the wave offering,
this the heave offering.

Waves
of earth passing
over you, into history.

You cling to the branch

the self offers.
It is slender. It is fragile.

Birds
flee from it
when you interrupt them
with your grasping
hands.

Children
die here, you know.
This is their only world.

THE ARRHYTHMIAS

Blank peal of a glass door in the archive of memory,
you want nothing or you fear nothing, breath is the daughter
you never had. Escape offers its temporary attention, gaze
set permanently on some middle distance at which a bridge
can be made out, dimly, to burn. I stepped onto
the archaeological site with a confidence borne of schematics

my soul had memorized. For this, yes, is the nature
of the soul, to recognize a pattern—& then respond
in the register of prisoners issued fresh new uniforms
one special day each year. They're so soft, as if
worn previously by angelic beings hunger had exterminated.
This is a poem about quiet, & the livid fractures

quiet binds, when, as Michael Palmer put it, "the heart
is flexible." We were sent down to the water table
to record the shadows of the curious animals, & the rings
they coveted. I dreamt terrible things in the deconsecrated
chapel, carried as if by a flood past vast banquets
my members had once attended, without my knowledge

or consent. Because a little knowledge is treacherous
like music, like the currencies of small republics, someone
makes it & we, fresh from the breath's actuarial seance,
press it into the album of the senses, desperate to act
before the officiant blows again on her bronze whistle.
I wanted to embark upon the natural history of glass

as someone else might an ocean liner, or a telephone call.
Why aren't the names of things determined by the tones
snow relinquishes as it strikes them, again & again?
Certain ecclesiastical languages must have a word for this,
Old Church Slavonic or Geez. The hospital corridors
seemed to revolve around some elusive definition of *fact,*

which annoyed me. Let's persuade the blind soldiers
to dance with their weapons, the heir apparent suggested,
adjusting his steel-rimmed spectacles. I have not forgotten
the taste shame left in the mouth of my childhood,
like bark stripped from some bitter tree & then infused,
delicately, with the aroma of a single ripe peach

I'd stolen. Sometimes it is good to steal the things
that already belong to you, like Christ or the long grass
that edged the columbarium's gravel promenade. Frost
trained its ship on the cage that held my bitter affections
until I knocked the zither from its sutured paws.
I wanted fire, I wanted to loosen all the little pegs that held

the theater fixed to the stallion's heaving, lathered flank.
Can I be honest with you, someone in the crowd kept asking.
Can I be an honest man in a vast shopping arcade
named for a war we lost, then won, then lost again.
The rain fed it & the memory of those vexed encampments
reproduced with phylogenetic accuracy. I excavated

a new forest from the shattered lens, but it demanded
that I carry it—I, who was just then entering the polis
from my dwelling in the outposts, on other business—
to age, for instance, to parley with the comity of my cells
which are programmed to receive time's emissaries
warmly, to stable their rough stock, accept their gifts.

They are all rigorous Platonists. Remember the island
where the dead were informed of their absolute right
to quit talking about philosophy, about both branding
& desire. Because that's what the dead, otherwise,
would insist upon discussing, on their endless late-night
radio programs sponsored by electricities we haven't yet

found the means to deplete. This poem is a discourse
on depletion, & on the joy I felt when, as a child, I latched
my purpose to the square, turquoise book entitled
The Sea, that belonged to my parents, in which black-
&-white photographs of diatoms taken at outrageous
magnifications mimed, or so I vaguely gathered,

their ten thousand benedictions. How strong the beams
seemed, then, billowing with the beatific intelligence
of magnetically charged objects. I wanted to be
a man of tribute, so I taught myself to walk, first,
& only then to speak. Because the body's movement
across a field of broken glass should mean something

the dead know about, when they approach the living,
rattling their begging bowls. All these modern grimoires
masquerading as loans to the confraternity of widows
whose spacious symbols admit the pilgrims
that arrive hourly from the desert, their maimed homilies,
their vitamin supplements, their ecstatic cries of praise.

CANTO SELAH

for & after Karen An-hwei Lee

There is no identical
sculpture
of silence, night's plane
edge pressed against
the upper
lip. You dress yourself
deep in the loss
of the moment, aspiring
to smelt
a cage from a star.
The grass is praying
in the capital
of grasses, which is lit
at both ends
like a city on fire.
It does not know tides.
It buries its face
in the shadow
of justice's flat well.
I warm my hands there
even
when the mirror
repeats its only curse,
which is
Son. Son. Son. Son.

A MEADOWLARK IN ARROW ROCK, MISSOURI
(Draft 1)

It is not insistent. It is not desperately clinging
               to the *is,* the *are.*
    It is familiar with the dusk.
(I write, "It is familiar with the dusk," words.)
    It does not call
        Do you believe, do you believe.
I don't know how much like a church it is
                  but the sun,
the sun if it knows worship clearly knows this,
        it reaches with its chasm
   towards the soft muscular throat, thinking
      Inside. There must be
an inside. It repeats this. Epochs chamber by.
I was stunned by the sheer scholarship of it.
    As well, the sound milk makes, or a sound
               milk might make.
Come away then, from the incision.
                 The wind
shot through the fence post like a knot of silk.
It is directly related to light, to the Pauline
               mission of light.
   Perhaps it is a preaching to the bees.
Scalded, pressing forward at the top of the wall,
    what does your soul say *now,*
           warden. Scars break
             beautifully
   in the early hours, you must be
awake to catch their fragments as they descend.

Some ashes of bees, kept reverently.
Little bits of Chopin on loan from adversity.
Memories of livestock filling the streets,
    archive them
            together with the bandages. What?
Yes, the new ones as well as the soiled ones.
And then: to bleed light, as if it were a key.
    Wound wound wound wound!
    The wonder of it, almost but not quite a lock.
                But it sounds better
        than *Hölderlin Hölderlin Hölderlin!*
which is perhaps the more accurate translation.

(Draft 2)

                Let's
memorize the darkness together, you & I.

SUFFERING

Someone is walking towards you. It's like in dreams—
only this is no dream—you know, you think you should know
who it is, but you can't say, the face is a blur, or your gaze
keeps glancing away from the face, or the figure is backlit
by some great light, the setting sun perhaps, leaving the visage
matte, a silhouette. The figure is closing the distance
between itself and you. It may be gesturing—its hands held out
towards you, or one hand, it could be waving, it could be
pointing, it could be a malediction. It could hold something
but if so, you can't make that something out. Did I mention
someone is walking towards you? Since it, the someone,
is backlit, its shadow streams towards you, gnomon
to the larger ebb and flow. You have, for the moment,
everything that's in your pockets, no more, no less: keys, pen,
wallet, a bit of neolithic flake picked up from the stream bed
behind a friend's house for no other reason than you
recognized it for what it was. You may be young. You may
be agèd. You're not sure, because you're watching someone
walking towards you: the sensible person asks is it someone
I know, or is it a stranger. There are so many people
in the world, aren't there? Say it, part of what lends music
its power is limitation. The same is true for verse, or the body,
by itself or in relation to other bodies. Did you have any pets?
is one of the questions the angels keep asking, and also the dead,
always so interested in the animals. Someone is walking
towards you now, and even if you don't acknowledge this fact,
the body registers the shift in the light, the slight modulation
of temperature, the way the red speeches of the politicians
no longer hold your attention, or not in the same way.
You wish, as you always wished, that someone would tell you

a story. But someone is walking towards you, this *is* the story,
you're in it. This is the rising action, it will take slightly longer
than you thought, you will not have time to learn French
or move to Texas, or, if you do, these things won't matter
in the ways you thought such things should matter,
like the death of Ovid which you recall from high school Latin,
the history of China or the proper method for manufacturing
steel. Or other things, the past, ceramic mugs. When I worked
in the prison we were instructed never to allow anyone
to explain what they did or didn't do. I broke that rule because
I, too, wanted someone to tell me a story. In this way
a little more night comes to rest inside the ship we call world,
the shadows of others grow a little longer. You know this,
because you've had time to study it. Is there a book
we can stow cruelty inside and leave it there, my student asked.
No, I told her. Because this is not about cruelty, and it's not
about pain. It's about you. What you're thinking,
what you're feeling now, real as cellos, the flag, as the viscosity
index of the secretions of aphids. It's about glass and blame.
It doesn't really matter what it is or isn't about, because someone
is walking towards you, someone is walking towards you now.

THE HOLY SPIRIT AS A VOWEL
IN EARLY SNOW (III)

It is, of course, unwritten, as in Hebrew.

The animals graze it, ekphrastically.

Evidently it distinguishes day from night.

One definition of *soul*
is that which swallows & swallows.

Israel, the lights, the illusions,
the neck of the sacrifice, which it loves.

All day I have been signing my name
to a pamphlet on grief,
is this all I can do, is this my capacity.

Milk, its homelessness,
two blind eyes staring. Is it sufficient.

It's much too late for any fiduciary
sense of loss, as it is of abandonment.

Small birds that seem to exist inside
or at the edge of earthly memory,
their hunger,
their rapid darts & feints: *look! look!*

The affirmation of the material world
which is not

a ladder, though it could be.
Screens painted in accordance with this
hung one, two, three
high up on the general's wall.

Listen: our imperfections, abundances.

Pray, pray for the peace of Jerusalem.

The shadows it casts at night
on monuments, on the general's wall.

EXODUS

after Jean Dubuffet

You could have said flame but you did not.
You could have said roof but did not.
You could have said light-bearing roof
beneath which a house crouches
you could have crushed pearls into powder
you could have struck a match.
You could have said prayer but you did not.

SOME LINES WRITTEN IN CLARE PRIORY YARD

I hurt myself into imagining. The flies, the priory flies,
settle over the length of my body, the blue of my shirt,
my vest. At one time I wanted music so badly I carved it
into the back of my left hand—the staff at least.
This was, notionally, to serve as a reminder. To carve
anything into the flesh, with any implement—the surgeons
do it, we (who survive) applaud. We (who are artists)
suspended. In the light of the priory yard, the fruits
of that labor, no longer visible (as they were, earlier,
under the awning of the pub). The flies avoid my skin,
prefer my shirt, its wavelength. All changed,
in the twinkling of an eye, but the wounds go with us.
Perhaps that is what attracts the flies, which do not ask
anything of me, save surface. Surface, the surface
of music, a guardian. It holds its crooked finger to its lips.
Sounds made by flies, spring warblers, rooks, the three
gardeners (two women, one man, all elderly) bearing
& then bearing away. Look, now I'm down on my hands
& knees, says one. But I am surfeited with looking.
I close my eyes. Such a great brightness reaches us.
In the walled courtyard of the priory I am a stranger,
but—a permitted stranger. In the absence left by music,
the world multiplies. In its presence also. I am,
in these moments, at the center of the world worlding.
Each fly, each jackdaw, each Austin friar, at the center:
a simultaneity of centers. Music threads us like a needle.
My garment sewn from scraps the dead pass through.
I don't mind, I am at rest among absolutes. To share,
to apportion: the great sum. Music in its measure. I lean

forward, I squint: Christ is still there. He measures
the distance, or—He is the distance, measured. It's true,
I thought I could sing my way to Him. Now I press
the back of my left hand to my dry lips. Some of this
was long ago; some of this is now. I spread my dreams
out on the priory lawn, to dry. There is a certain peace
in being a guest among guests. The world, worlding,
falls away—a bit, to a respectful distance. Then I hear
the siren of the ambulance, rushing as if towards
me, towards where I am, but veering off, somewhere
to the north. My friend says we are almost done
with these expressions of faith. It does not grieve him.
We must start over, he says. With what, I ask.
With small, informal associations grounded in friendship,
he replies. Friend hand. Friend breath. Friend rook.
Friend pain. The world cries *Welcome welcome welcome
welcome!* It is wildly indiscriminate. One gardener,
two pass me with their wheelbarrows. Don't mind me,
I want to say. They don't mind me. This is my belonging-
place. The blue of my shirt, the same blue as this late
April sky—perhaps this is what confounds the flies.
Friend fly, spinning your decimals. In season of patronage.
Tithe of the material, stored in the soul's broad barn.
I replenish my testimony. The Christ of *here,*
vs. the Christ of *there* (there, in the visible distance,
beckoning, unbeckoning). This song is a measurement
I wake into. Its consciousness which, being song,
is a musical consciousness, a set of relationships.
A woman passing says, to her lover, That's my favourite,
the one I always give away. She says, I'm not so proud....

The bearing-away, vs. the giving-away. Music does both.
Mind does both. Spirit embraces these motions.
To relinquish. To rise, into the ember of the now:
blow on it, watch it glow. It seems to do this silently
but, since it is matter, I assume it makes some sound,
however imperceptible. I am scoring the sound
of that glow for rooks, ambulance, & passing aircraft,
with warbler canticle. And three gardeners at their labors.
I will never know their names. I am astonishingly
at peace with this, as with the certainty of my death.
The flies must sense this, somehow. They have come
to anoint—if not my body, then at least my shirt,
its woven proxy, that the sky dies into. But really
this is a poem of life (as death is always & only a poem
of life). It submits itself to matter, & to the measurements
of matter. A waking-into. A music mutually intelligible
to all parties, living & dead. Thus the Resurrection
enacts its one true miracle play, a recurring mummery.
I lift it to my moistened lips while Christ watches.
As for my friends, they are all far away. I miss them.
The missing, as my preceptor (now dead) once wrote,
grows large between us. I hurt myself into imagining—
their lives, what they are doing right now; my life,
other lives. These altars. The belief in appearances,
alongside the belief in the essential falsity of appearances,
superimposed. We, the superimposures. Accidental
(I mean in the musical sense). I am fully present,
but also insufficiently. I, who would never be mistaken
for a gardener (especially by other, natural gardeners).
Right there, where the Christ of Christ is standing,

free of scars but fresh of wounds. The music is drawn
into the wounds, it disappears into them. The gaze
is drawn into the wounds, it disappears into them.
The hand—but no, the hand pauses. It's right here.
It flaunts itself, helplessly. It wants to call music to itself,
to its etched staff, but it can't, because it has no lips,
no mouth, no cords, no tongue. Is the hand a wound?
The hand as both a unit & a means of measurement.
I am using it now, to the extent damage allows.
I measure the distant Christ, the new church, the great
yew, the yellowhammer's palpitating throat hovering
just before me. While the flies go on measuring me,
rapt. They have so little time. They press their bodies
into the pattern of the parched weave of my shirt,
their new nation. What must that be like, to nation?
In this, my belonging-place, where I remain a stranger
among strangers, admonishing the stranger-sun.

MARCHING BEAR GROUP

Effigy Mounds National Monument

The earth is a tongue. The breath, likewise. The mowers,
old friends, also here in due season—now fled from me.
But not my friend wind. Not my friend tongue.
They rise to the mutual. Or they follow one another
as in a long queue, tongue-to-wind, breath-to-tongue.
I dreamt my way here, through a distant illness.
We are a long way from the war, or so we prefer to think.
The war, that brought us here: *O sustaining war.*
I bow my head, not in prayer but in shame.
Shame, something the earth can't know. But prayer,
it's something the land receives, something the land
listens for, even though it (the land) remains unaddressed.
This land understands the postures of prayer.
It shifts beneath me in minuscule ways. The water table
shifts, the deep roots of the prairie grasses shift.
I'm a sojourner, temporary in ways we rather hope
they aren't. I pass through the tallgrass tunnel, a rebirth
of sorts. Where the military power once passed,
streaming west. I imagine this although I don't want to.
I want to imagine the prairie grasses in their long waking
which is also their long sleep. To sleep & wake
simultaneously: something else this ground knows
that I don't & can't. *Shelter,* a pause in the indivisible.
All the way down, all the way down (insist the voices
when I tune to them). I grow older here, just watching.
I wrote, at the time, *We will beat the fantastic messengers
to the Capitol. We will take the shortcut through
the new forest & the old forest. Among the animals....*

& I was right about all that, only tragically:
we *were* the animals. We were there in our animal
skins, with our animal tongues, our animal breaths
(that we share with others, the smallest lives).
We climbed the low embankments as we can do here,
although it seems more prudent not to. It seems
prudent, somehow, to refuse. *Occupation,* somehow
different from what the trees do, although they, too, exist
in space, they root, they anchor. I am abashed
in the presence of these interments (and divers others).
I reach out to a black walnut as if this is something
we could discuss. Of course we can't. At the Capitol,
the animals running into & among other animals;
here, in procession, a stately motion, geological.
Because the animals (some animals) wanted it this way:
perhaps they felt it was prudent, perhaps they had some idea
of this thing we call prudence, of place. I have an idea
& am thankful that it, & I, are very small. I move
bipedally, on my own two legs, ascending through groves
that are tended, as in some Old Testament parable.
Always a puzzle: whether to tend the groves or not,
cut them down, let them grow as they would (as they do)
on their own. The military road, now little more than a path,
leads away from the bluff. & here are the tenders,
quite suddenly, with their loud machines! I doff my hat.
Tenders of the grasses, of the groves, I salute you,
I salute my idea of you (a small idea), that is, of your labor.
There is a god in this, true, but this god is a god of men
which is to say, of ideas & of works. He is a breath.

94

He is a tongue. *The sound of a going in the tops*
of the mulberry trees, as one source puts it, anapestically:
also, & not incidentally, a prelude to war. So I call out
to the war (once the mowers & tenders have gone)—
I shout *War!* It's an invitation, but I hear only my own
voice faintly (did I imagine it?) at large in the maze,
the sleeping beasts of the earth, almost plowed down
but outlined in rough herbage the tenders manicure.
In procession towards...what, I wonder. & so I follow:
to a gate at the end of the glade that opens
(if I were to open it, which I do not) into a plowed field,
the blank agricultural logic we pillaged towards.
I observe the field. I want to follow the field, but how
does one follow a field? Once I mended fences around
such a field. This was in Kansas, & I mended badly.
I also sawed off & poisoned the Osage orange saplings
that had sprung up there. I did this for a friend,
with his son. His son started at one edge of the field
& I started at the other & we met, of course, in the middle
where meetings can happen. It was cold, then.
I had stains on my hands, which were likewise cold,
from the poison. My friend's son asked me some questions
about God, there, in the middle of the field, & I tried
to answer them. Now, here, at the edge of this ark,
at the edge of the gathering field, I ask no questions, &
I answer none. I turn my back on the field & photograph
the animals, both the living & those in the earth.
It turns out they're difficult to capture in photography,
these earthfast animals, the ones my species constructed

either before, during, or after another war.
They appear slight (which they are not). They appear
undulant (which they are). They appear dismissible,
& that's an open question: does one dismiss
or does one not? I don't feel dismissed, here. I feel
presenced. To the presence that dwells inside presence,
the presence that wind knows, that breath knows.
The tongue doesn't know, but it prays, it tries so hard.
It prays to the presence it doesn't know, that passes
over it, sometimes in the form of that agon, the voice.
Because the voice is a god to the mute tongue.
It comes, from the tongue's point of view—its fleshwork—
from somewhere else, some deeper place. The tongue
is often quite accurate inside its blind cave
against which the shadow-figures stretch & move.
The mouth is small. Diameter, a measure of inclusion
the tongue brokers. But my tongue is wounded
(a phrase I never found in any language primer I consulted)
& so my call, my voice, remains unanswered.
At the Capitol the animals are photographed & filmed
striking other animals, & making the noises that animals
make. I was ever a student of the noises of animals,
how can they make so many different sounds?
In my youth I practiced, I studied under professionals
who were responsible for making the very best animal
sounds. I opened my mouth wide, at new angles;
I tried to imagine my tongue in different places, places
the tongue had no desire to go. There was an art
to this, & I won't lie, I coveted it. I coveted it

with all the desire an animal can muster.
This was pure belief, according to the doctrine of tongues.
St. Thomas, make your oratory here, precisely here
is what I want to say, where the wounds can find you.
But that's not the right story, is it? I take a breath,
hold it, release it as if it were, in fact, an animal.
It bounds away from me, into the aging trees.
Soon they will fall, even with the best care we can offer,
& men with chainsaws will come to dismember them
& haul them away. Later, in winter, someone
will perhaps light a fire & they will pare a new debt
as they combust. This is an ascension, the one
animals dream of, when animals dream, or as in waking
I plunge into. I reach down to the animals in the earth
as if I had something to teach them, but I don't.
I place my hand against one, then another, because
what my hand wants, right now, is to be a substitute
for war. The war that brought it here. The adductive war.
The war that makes the palm itch & the fingers clench.
The wars among the animals that the winds buffet.
The war in which I find a voice, which is myself, at dusk.

AFTERNOON SNOW, COLLEGEVILLE

I sometimes think I am an artificer of winter.

You, you there, help me,
hold this instrument. Only in certain films
is it used as a weapon.
Here, we use it to cut holes in the solid dark.

The prescriptive urgency
illuminating the earth's bespoke manuscript
convalesces, or so it seems.

Without thinking, prayer resembles itself.

Without thinking, the body's
memory (I mean its palimpsest) goes unread.

All rise, into nation. Repetition is simply
a means to glass, its end.

I bury beauty in it, I spread out my wares
on blankets for passers-by to ogle.

Everything requires an edge,
according to Böhme, including Paradise.

I place winter there, I trim it
so that the birds will notice it, its marvelous
hyphens
they collect as souvenirs.

Not fire (for who or what can collect fire?).

The proof will be my body,
Louise Glück wrote. By which she meant,
matter is never alone.

I work winter as it works me, heavy-handed.

For this was ever a song of my lovers.

Gather yourselves, partisans,
friends. I await you (& every future trace).
The dead prevail, as they do every time.
They pull the lake's frosted margin
to their many mouths, which is how we see

them: a consummation.
Not a forefeast, & not the common loss.

IN THE DESIGNED LANDSCAPE (GARDEN OF PLANES)

Bloedel Reserve

O you rakers of sand, come. I bow, slightly, to the stone ear. It is once again
the season of resemblances. Forfeit, my life, your life, lives lived
in the company of doors. Come in, come in, the sound is moist with morning dew.
It will perform to your bidding. The party guests are old men & women now,
or dead. One thrust an awl through his childhood. The awl was language,
he had heated it, it glowed reddish-orange. So much for the dead—you, rakers of sand,
I am talking to you. I invite you in. You may blow out your candles & deposit them

here, in this iron box. Archipelagoes circling the hotel at midnight, I watched
through dulled blinds. I breathed onto the cold porcelain as if it were glass,
as if through it I might see the shapes & faces of the departed. Fall through friendship
& become visible, I was counseled. The moss adhering to the pyramids'
four planes, or else not adhering, & for that they were removed, presumably destroyed.
In the photograph children swam here as children do, untethered in the moment
from what they have already come to think of as the weight of their bodies. But no,

it's merely redistributed in the way that joy, giving way to sorrow, is merely
redistributed, that is, within the body, among its limbs & organs. Into & back out
of the *marvelous labyrinth*. I arrived here as one with precedents, as one
whose heart beats unrhythmically, a staggered tattoo as if it knew it was misspelling
some word, some very important word, over & over again but was powerless
to stop. I speak to my heart, to comfort it, a little, while I wait for the rakers of sand.
They are late, it seems. Perhaps they are occupied elsewhere. At this hour

the earth reveals itself as a succession of planes. What is signal vs. what is noise,
the fox that speeds by, late to its den. I want stone to be holy & so it is,
even crushed, gravel, sand. I watched the film of the cathedral falling again & again
in my dream. It was ringed with animals, at a respectful distance of course,

you could feel their quietness when the camera panned towards them. The psalms,
sketches for patterns a language could make. I am both here & not-here,
among the machines & those who operate them, my dawnside kin. In the earliest light

they resemble small bits of leftover steel. Their visibility is measurable. My pain,
what I experience as pain, also measurable, or so I am told. The yes unfolded
into the no that unfolds into a larger yes. The doctrine of planes,
it was preached here, do you not remember, o rakers of sand? But no, you came later,
in the absence of frontiers. You blended a silence back into the war, where no one
could find it unless everyone could. So we gathered at the shoreline
where the wrecked ship was burning. I may have told you this before, the tiny seizures

the horses' breaths made in the chill air. I asked what this word meant, *citizen,*
what brand this was, settling into new skin. I heard the great doors close,
I had my back to them. O rakers of sand, understand me! I had forfeited nothing,
I dwelt—then—quite comfortably in the cell of my eye. You step out of the stone
& into a psalm, yes, that much is true, really it is unavoidable, like the image
of the orphan sleeping among beasts. I, a beast among beasts, am present, slow
as the memory everything is becoming. I latch & I lapse. I am meant to wait here,

to wait *waitingly,* by which we mean, contemplation. I carry the chill
in my long bones like the fingernail of a saint gathered—one of millions—
from a rocky beach. Pared so carefully, or perhaps torn by violence & only later
rounded by the action of the waves. Rakers of sand, your new shadows
become you, I must say. Perhaps you are now playing cards
in the planetarium, perhaps you are crossing to where I am, where I await you.
I have wagered all my lenses for a ghost, on behalf of ghosts—I am,

as I told the docent, part-ghost myself. The long apprenticeship, what of it.
We are, after all, subject to ideas, to the tyranny of ideas. I cast my consequence
here, in parallel staves; perhaps it will draw some music to it. This is the perfection
of the untranslatable element, where the red-orange goes when the awl cools.
It rests, then, lightly in the hand, the way night rests also & so lightly in the hand.
Night, that memory without consequence recurring, like the blessing
pronounced at the end of an annual feast. It isn't so difficult, being part-ghost—

the animals in particular seem to accept me just a bit more freely. It places me
in a different relationship to alms, to charity. O rakers of sand, close
your geography textbooks, bow your heads if you must, rise from your long tables—
it is time for you to come, to me, I mean, to where I stand. I am the calendar
behind the calendar, unstripping the days like flames imprisoned in a lamp.
I brighten, I darken, I who narrate the cracks in the prophecies,
who pierced my own childhood with memory, over & over again until it seemed

it was all eyes peering from the great dark garment breath had prepared
for me. The doors, I open & close them, they remember, that is their other ministry.
The encirclement, what can we know of it, we place it in our mouths
not for the taste but because we suspect the tongue might know, the tongue
has a way of knowing the depths to which both water & sand descend, the tongue
is at home there, *beneath,* placed against stone, the stone lips, the stone mouth,
the stone eye, the stone ear that listens, o rakers of sand, citizens, citizens.

NOTES & ACKNOWLEDGMENTS

Gratitude to the editors of the following journals in which poems from this collection previously appeared:

American Poetry Review: "Fountains Abbey, Pentecost," "In the Designed Landscape (Garden of Planes)"
Beloit Poetry Journal: "On the Senses"
Bennington Review: "Grievance," "Saint Sauveur"
Blackbird: "Canto Selah"
Cincinnati Review: "The Arrhythmias," "[The Healing Loom]"
Georgia Review: "Suffering"
Harvard Review: "And the Stonesquarers"
Image: "To a Shelf Fungus in Acadia National Park," "I Am the Vine"
Iowa Review: "Acadia Winter Poem"
Massachusetts Review: "A Meadowlark in Arrow Rock, Missouri"
The Nation: "In the Epoch of Bronze"
New American Writing: "The Holy Spirit as a Vowel in Early Snow" (I, II, III), "Afternoon Snow, Collegeville"
New England Review: "Houses Built from the Bodies of Lions or of Dogs," "Some Lines Written in Clare Priory Yard"
Paris Review: "Suite for A.W.N. Pugin"
Ploughshares: "Tarry"
Poetry: "Mount Grace Priory"
Poetry Review (UK): "Effigy Mounds National Monument"
Posit: "Exodus"
Times Literary Supplement (UK): "Contemplating the Pippa Blackall Millennium Window at Alpheton Church"
Waxwing: "Creation Myth Suite"
Yale Review: "At the George Caleb Brigham House," "To Each Light of Which I Am a Brother"

"Tarry," "Canto Selah," "Fountains Abbey (Pentecost)," and "At the George Caleb Bingham House" were reprinted in William Wright et al., eds., *The Southern Poetry Anthology, Vol. IX: Virginia* (Texas University Press, 2022). "Tarry" was also reprinted in Bill Henderson, ed., *Pushcart Prize XLII: Best of the Small Presses* (W.W. Norton & Co., 2023).

The Acadia-based poems were written during an Artist-in-Residence fellowship at Acadia National Park: many thanks to the park, its rangers, and especially program officer Jay Elhard for maintaining this program, one of the oldest of its kind. Thanks also to the mostly invisible (to me) caretakers and rangers at Effigy Mounds National Monument.

Arrow Rock is an all-but-ghost town on the Missouri River in west-central Missouri, established in 1829 on the Santa Fe Trail. Since 1926 it has been a state historic landmark and since 1963 a national historic landmark. George Caleb Bingham (1811–1879) was a Missouri artist lauded for his contributions to 19th-century American painting (as well as social documentation through painting). The Bingham House and the Big Spring are now owned by the State of Missouri, and the (former) Arrow Rock Christian Church and (former) African American lodge hall by the Friends of Arrow Rock, a nonprofit preservation organization. Thanks to the Friends of Arrow Rock and to the historic site staff for their hospitality. Thanks likewise to Jan Chism Wright, the Brownville Historical Society, and the Brownville Fine Arts Association for assistance in Brownville, Nebraska.

A.W.N. Pugin (1812–1852) was a Victorian architect known for his revival of the Gothic style in the United Kingdom. The biography in question was Rosemary Hill's *God's Architect: Pugin and the Building of Romantic Britain* (London: Allen Lane, 2007; New Haven: Yale University Press, 2009). In the poem it says "Pugin," but it's really a deep bow to Anne Carson.

"In the Designed Landscape (Garden of Planes)" refers to a partially-destroyed work of landscape art on the grounds of what is now the Bloedel Reserve on Bainbridge Island, Washington, by Richard Haag (1923-2018). It is also an elegy for Tomas Tranströmer (1931–2015), whom it quotes; Theodore Roethke (1908-1963), who drowned in the swimming pool Haag's installation replaced; and three generations of workers, mostly Japanese immigrants, who tended the gardens there, most notably under the direction of Fujitaro Kubota (1879–1973).

The title "I Have Touched His Wealth with the Certainty of Experience" is drawn from Simone Weil's letter of 26 May 1942 to Father Joseph-Marie Perrin, reproduced in *Waiting for God*. The exact quotation (in Emma Craufurd's translation) is "I do not need any hope or promise in order to believe that God is rich in mercy. I know this wealth of his with the certainty of experience; I have touched it."

Thanks to the Bloedel Reserve and the Collegeville Institute at St. John's University for residencies in 2020; to Clare Hall at the University of Cambridge, where I was a visiting fellow in 2021; and to Yaddo. Thanks to Karen An-hwei Lee, Sasha Dugdale, Kaveh Akbar, and Sasha Steensen for their kind endorsements, and to John Lane. As always, gratitude to friends who served as readers for all or parts of this book at various stages in its development: Dana Levin, Bruce Beasley, Victoria Chang, Dan Beachy-Quick, and Shane McCrae.